Light as a Feather

Mary Jo Varn

ISBN 978-1-64416-044-2 (paperback)
ISBN 978-1-64416-045-9 (digital)

Copyright © 2018 by Mary Jo Varn

All rights reserved. No part of this publication may be reproduced, distributed, or transmitted in any form or by any means, including photocopying, recording, or other electronic or mechanical methods without the prior written permission of the publisher. For permission requests, solicit the publisher via the address below.

Christian Faith Publishing, Inc.
832 Park Avenue
Meadville, PA 16335
www.christianfaithpublishing.com

Printed in the United States of America

I believe in signs, "God incidences," and listening to that little voice in my heart. With that being said, I would like to share a story that would change my life and the lives of others forever.

December 8, 2011, started out as a normal day full of possibilities, and a calmness wafted over me. I had been retired for three months and enjoyed having some much-needed free time. Today, I was headed to Mass with my parents to celebrate the feast of the Assumption, the day that Mary discovers she is about to become the mother of Jesus. Little did we know that morning that our situation later that day would be a direct contrast to that Feast Day.

Our daughter, Jacquie, and her husband, Brian, were due to have their much-anticipated baby on January 3, 2012. There were many showers, countless trips made to the local Babies "R" Us store, especially by my husband, Dennis, the way over-the-top grandpa-to-be. Excitement was certainly in the air, but as thrilled as I was, there was always a feeling in my heart that made me a little more cautious, for whatever reason. Sometimes I would just get these funny feelings inside, telling me not to get too excited.

I would get mad at myself because Jacquie had been feeling great throughout most of her pregnancy. She took good care of herself, read books on pregnancy, and attended every childbirth-information class available. One of later classes mentioned that, if you weren't feeling the baby move much, it might be cause for concern.

She immediately took that to heart, and whenever Brian spoke to "Bunco," as they lovingly called the baby, they would in turn receive a nice kick. I assured her that later in my two pregnancies, I had not felt the baby move and kick as much. I remember being slightly annoyed with the instructor for worrying my very conscientious daughter.

Jacquie and Brian were scheduled at three thirty to have their appointment and routine ultrasound that afternoon, and I was anxiously awaiting the outcome. I decided to finally wash some of the baby clothes that I had been procrastinating to do and was loading them into the dryer around three o'clock and, unfortunately, got one of my little feelings that something might be wrong. As the phone rang at 4:15 p.m., Dennis took the call from our sobbing daughter that there was no heartbeat found during the routine ultrasound. My worst fears coming true: their sweet baby was gone.

In that blur of the conversation, she told us to pick up my parents and make the longest drive ever to their home forty minutes away. Our son, Dan, was also called along with Brian's parents, Vicki and Jimmy. I was so relieved that both Jacquie and Brian wanted family around at this most difficult time in their lives, as they could have shut as all out, literally holed up in their room. As we all gathered together, I know God was there enfolding us all in his loving embrace. That had to be the case; otherwise, the grief would have been too much to bear. We were all in shock, but we were together.

There was no rhyme or reason at that point why the baby's heart had stopped. Shock waves trickled around the doctor's office, and they were told to be at the hospital the next day for either a normal labor/delivery and have nature take its course or a possible cesarean section. Our main concern now was for our daughters' health. We had unthinkably lost our grandbaby, but could not bear the thought of anything happening to our daughter. The thought of having to wait, possibly for days, to deliver was inconceivable.

That night was endless, and needless to say, a sleepless one. All I could think of doing was to sit at the computer to write a mass email to all our family and dear friends to start praying. The words seemed to come from someone other than myself. I explained that my daughter had become a vehicle for an angel that God apparently needed, but questionably, more than we did. That was the only thing that made sense to me, in the blur that was occurring in my life right then. It actually gave me a sense of peace as I know God gave me that wisdom and peace.

We made the hour trek to the hospital early the next morning after (of course) going to the wrong facility initially as it was not a local hospital we were familiar with. Understandably, we were very distraught and nervous as we entered Jacquie's room. But as soon as we were in there, I knew in my heart, we were in the hands of God.

A nurse (whom we know now was an angel sent to us) was on her knees holding Jacquie's hand. She was explaining to her and Brian what all that was to happen that day. Joan Marie was very kind and compassionate as she looked into my daughter's fearful eyes, and her presence seemed to calm us all down. At that point, the couple was still in shock and not sure of the proper thing to do when asked if they would like to "meet" their child. Jacquie truthfully admitted she was not sure how to answer that question.

Then Joan Marie said the words that would be the turning point of this whole ordeal: "Sometimes you have to say hello before you can say goodbye."

It was one of those "lightbulb" moments.

Jacquie then said, "Of course, we will meet and hold our baby. It's not their fault."

It was so evident to all of us then. Of course, we all wanted to meet the baby we had been anticipating and wanting for so many months. Joan Marie gave us the clarity none of us close to the situation could muster before. She was the first of the wonderful people whom God would bring to help us.

The hospital chaplain was kind and considerate, giving Jacquie tips of calmly breathing using visualization. A friend of my aunt's named Roger, who was a deacon in the church Jacquie and Brian attended but did not know personally came to the hospital after hearing the story. Roger had lost a granddaughter due to an illness and understood our pain, our loss. He would explain to us how they coped. It was so reassuring at that point to meet someone who had experienced the same circumstances. You start to feel like you are a member of a club that no one should ever have to join. But out of this meeting, we would develop a tradition that we carry on to this day. Roger explained that his wife came up with the idea of the "Courtney candle." The candle, named after their granddaughter, was present at every family event and holiday. It is burned in her memory and a reminder that she is with the family during these special times. We thought it was an excellent idea and was so healing for us.

Our dear parish priest from St. Anthony's in Canton, Ohio, would make the near-hour drive to be with us that morning and most of the day. He took time out of his very busy day to be with us, and his presence was calming and reassuring for us all. In the midst of a lot of hurting, there was a calmness and almost sanctity in the hours to come.

The doctor arrived shortly and was explaining to us, Brian's parents, Dan, and Father Tom what was to occur next. He was visibly upset as he was as just as surprised as we all were. Jacquie's pregnancy was textbook, normal, and an easy one. He said that he looked over and over her medical records for any red flags he may have missed, but there were none. His sincere apology and kindness, along with professionalism, struck me. He was so compassionate, and we found out why—his wife too had had a miscarriage. We had met yet another member of "the club" that was brought there to support us.

After examining Jacquie extensively, it was decided that Jacquie was to have a C-section. As relieved as I was that the birth would be over soon instead of letting nature take its course, we all, as parents, were now concerned with Jacquie's health and well-being, first and foremost. The excellent nursing staff took her back to the delivery room, after we all said nervous I-love-yous, gave kisses, and said prayers led by Father Tom. Brian would go back to the delivery room also for the surgery. His love and support for Jacquie were so evident, even though the hurt and fear was insurmountable for him as well.

The trek for us all to the cafeteria was a quiet one. We made idle chitchat over coffee, but our minds and hearts were all in the delivery room. The only thing normal about waiting for this baby to be born was the anticipation of the sex and name, as it was always kept a secret. About an hour passed, and as we made our way to the waiting room, we got the call; the delivery was completed. We met Brian outside the waiting room with the good news Jacquie was fine, and all went well, thanks be to God. Our sweet angel was a little girl. We all cried with tears of sadness, relief and joy—all at the same time.

"What's the name, what's the name?" we questioned as we never could eke it out of the couple during the whole pregnancy.

"No," he said, "you have to wait for Jacquie."

As they wheeled her out of the delivery room to us, a wave of relief passed through Dennis and I. We were thanking God privately that our daughter was all right. Now we could grieve our granddaughter.

As we were all standing together around the bed back in her room, my mother had joined us as my nieces, Bridget and Mary, had brought her to the hospital. Wild horses could not have kept her home. As Joan Marie handed this sweet angel to Jacquie and Brian, in a pink crocheted hat and sweater that the hospital ministry had provided, we were all taken aback by her beauty and delicate features. She had her dad's cute nose and—laughingly, the nurses said—big feet. I could see the resemblance of my daughter some twenty-eight years prior, when I held her for the first time: the strawberry-blonde hair and the long fingers that I was positive would belong to a world-famous concert pianist. We were told prior to this that the umbilical cord was wrapped around her neck four times, so we were unsure how this would affect her looks. But she was perfect and looked only like she was sleeping.

"This is Lily Jo," my daughter announced, a delicate name for the delicate flower she was holding. "The Jo is for you, Mom."

Her name was Lily Jo. At this announcement, I was taken aback and had to smile all at the same time.

My maiden name was Martino, so growing up I had a rhyming name—Mary Jo Martino. I always asked my mom why. I was half joking, but of course, I knew the story; it had been told to me since I could remember. I was adopted at eight days old by my wonderful parents on March 18, 1957. She had always promised the Blessed Virgin Mary in prayer, that if she was ever to have a daughter, the name was to be in her honor. My mother was so very excited as she got the call about the adoption that she got confused, thinking it was the feast day of St. Joseph, which is March 19—hence the name, rhyming or not, Mary Jo. Apparently, Jacquie always loved hearing that story, so when she married Brian Crescenzo a year prior, the wheels were in motion that if they had a daughter, the Jo and the rhyming tradition would live on. Growing up as an adopted child in the 1950s, I had what my mom called a "gray" adoption. Everything was legal, but my parents, especially my mother, always worried that my birth parents would come and try to take me back. After eleven years of marriage, and years of wanting a child—with many disappointments along the way—her nervousness was very understandable. She was not taking any chances that I was going away, *ever*. I was very much loved, and a known fact, overprotected. But as I parent and grandparent myself now, I totally understand and am so very grateful for all the love I was showered with. So my mother made up a song—a song she taught me, at the age of two, to sing *loudly*, if by some chance, any one ever came for me. (Although, they would have had to knock both my parents out first.)

"Who is this pretty little girl? Mary Jo, Mary Jo, Mary Jo Martino."

Since Jacquie had always loved the story and the song, when it was time to print out a program for a service in a few days, Lily Jo's song was most certainly included: "Who is this pretty little girl I know? Lily Jo, Lily Jo, Lily Jo Crescenzo."

As we made a circle around Jacquie's bed, we all held hands, and Father Tom led a beautiful prayer service and blessed Lily Jo. It was a sad and beautiful moment all at once, and as people always say, surreal. You could feel the love in that room so strongly—so much that Joan Marie, who was holding my hand, told me how honored she was to be a part of it. She complimented us and admitted the nursing staff admired how well our family was handling this sad situation. I was overcome with emotion and gratefulness at her words, but knew in my heart that God was there. He was helping all of us, making us strong. I felt at that point that he had a plan. He was giving us his grace that would get us all through this difficult time.

The hospital had kindly assigned Jacquie to a room in an alcove secluded from other rooms on the maternity floor, and most importantly, the nursery. Her room was a revolving door full of friends and relatives that came and went continuously. Jacquie and Brian wanted and needed to be surrounded by everyone, and that is how they were coping and healing.

It came time for Jacquie to be dismissed, but not before meeting with Don, the funeral director. It is always such a hard process in any situation, but this was even more difficult. But his professionalism and kindness made it easier. And again, God had his hand in this situation as well. Don and his wife had lost a child also. Everyone who had a major part dealing with Jacquie and Brian had lost a child. The irony was too evident to dismiss.

They agreed to a small private ceremony at the Wadsworth cemetery with immediate family, and Lily's godparents, Matt and Kristin, who the kids went to Kent State with.

Deacon Roger was the celebrant, and of course, Don handled all the arrangements. He even made a program that included "Lily Jo's Song" printed on it, after he heard the story. He later presented all of us with necklaces with Lily Jo's footprint on them. It is treasure we all cherish today.

We all got through the service with God's help, and then had a meal together at a local restaurant. The hardest part, however, has to be when everyone goes home and life is supposed to go "back to normal". Life is never normal again, but becomes a "new normal" that you have to get used to.

Den and I were going back and forth to Wadsworth every day since that fateful Thursday, and wanted to spend as much time together and helping however we could. Again, we were blessed that Jacquie and Brian's healing process included being with people. Friends were so kind in sending cards, flowers, gifts, and visits with them. Kristin organized homemade meals to come to their home for weeks.

When I was home, we too received many cards, gifts and support from so many people. Many were understandably at a loss for words, but somehow Den and I could deal with it all. Don't think for a minute we were not devastated, but again, we got the courage to even console others. We had friends admit they never even considered something like this could ever happen to them, and they had been blessed with many grandchildren. I truly believe this tragedy opened people's minds and hearts in a way only the death of an infant could. Also, Christmas was nearing, and everyone seems typically to be more sentimental around that time of year.

I must interject here. As devastating as it was losing Lily Jo at birth, we were all comforted in the fact that we were spared the agony of losing her after having her for a few hours or even days, and we are forever grateful for that. We felt attached to her the minute we met her, albeit only briefly. Our hearts ached as we got our short "hello" in preparation for the long goodbye. We cannot even fathom parents and grandparents who have babies brought to them with issues, knowing they will eventually lose them. So many stories were told to us of people who had dealt with miscarriages and losses of children that we never knew about, until this happened in our family.

As I spoke to a dear friend during this time, she mentioned to me that after she received my sad news earlier in the week, she went to tell her husband. She looked down, and coming out of his sweater, was a tiny white feather. It struck her that it looked like an "angel feather." I recall I was comforted by this conversation. A few hours later, as I was cleaning the stove top, there was the same tiny white angel feather Theresa mentioned, lying in the corner of my stove! I can remember being taken aback. What was the chance of finding the same type of feather a few hours later? I saved it as a reminder of the special coincidence. Little did I know then, it was the start of something exceptional for us.

We also lost two uncles December 21 and 24. Three very special people were brought into heaven that month. We somehow got through the very different holidays that 2011 had to offer, but it was also a start of a lovely tradition that we still enjoy today.

As I mentioned prior, deacon Roger's family burned their Courtney candle at special family gatherings. We introduced our "Lily luminary" on Christmas Eve. A friend of mine had given me a white metal angel candleholder that I used many years. I had put it away and truthfully forgot about it until I found it in a cupboard upstairs. It was perfect. You can change the votive candle to celebrate any occasion. It was front and center on the holiday table, with the reminder for all that Lily Jo was there with us on Christmas and has been there on all occasions ever since. It was these little things that helped us cope, something as simple as a candle holder.

Time has a way of marching on, and life has a way of continuing on. It was a new year, 2012. For whatever reason, I started thinking of Lily as I would walk out our bedroom door. I could envision her as a little girl flitting around the corner. And that is where I found my next two surprises, two feathers the morning of January 2, in the corner right outside my door.

We all knew Jacquie's due date of January 4 would be a very difficult one. I decided to do something to take my mind off it. So I decided to take down the Christmas tree. I finished up and swept the floor. Later that day, I saw something glistening in the corner. A wing from an angel ornament was on the floor. I had broken the ornament before Christmas, and certainly had been around the tree area many times since to clean it then, and afterwards as well. We had company around the tree many times as well. And now, here was an angel wing on Lily's due date! It was another comforting sign that something special was happening …

Feathers were coming to me more frequently during the next few months, as I seemed to find them wherever I went. They were found in stores, parking lots, and on my daily walk; even once when I opened a carton of strawberries, there was one lying on top! It seemed like I was a feather magnet. Each time I would find one, I would get so excited and know Lily was speaking to me. I started collecting all shapes, sizes, and colors of feathers in a bag. Of course, I mentioned it to the family, and eventually, feathers were now appearing to Jacquie and our son, Dan. They would pop up on special days for them like birthdays, or when something big was happening in their life. So far, I had about thirty after receiving my first feather.

I was so caught up in the joy and wonder of finding these treasures that I starting telling my friends and acquaintances about my findings. Some people looked at me sympathetically, or like I really was a wacko. Normally, I am a pretty sensitive person and would get my feelings hurt, and just stop talking. Not in this situation! It seemed that I became bolder when it came to our Lily and the signs I was receiving. But for as many people who looked at me as if I was a crazy woman, there were ten times more people who believed me. It would spark a conversation of hearing about people who also received pennies, dimes, feathers, bird visits, especially from cardinals. People were so willing to share these stories with me, and it was a great relief to all parties involved, especially me. It was like a little sorority of people who lost loved ones, who shared these signs and stories with each other. I feel that that was my place in this journey. I am blessed to know a lot of people, and I think God knew that I would be able to spread the "good news," so to speak, of hope, and that those from heaven really are trying to communicate with us here on earth.

The doctor had wanted Jacquie and Brian to wait at least six months before trying to conceive another child. They were very anxious to have another baby, but Lily Jo would always be their first child. They talked to and about her often. I was so happy that this little life was remembered in the best possible way. They went to the cemetery every Sunday after church, not to be sad, but to talk to her. It became a part of their routine, and they were amazing and a true inspiration. One Sunday in May, they were visiting and spotted some clover by her headstone. Jacquie recalled talking to Lily and asked if she could send her a four-leaf clover. She had never seen one in person and thought it would be pretty neat. That following Friday, Jacquie was in her office, where she is a school psychologist. A boy came in and told her he was having a bad day, and that his friend gave him something to feel better. He then proceeded to put a four-leaf clover on her desk. Her guardian angel, unbeknown to us, was setting the wheels in motion.

In early June, we rented a house in Emerald Isle, North Carolina. The room we had designated for Brian and Jacquie was upstairs. A sign greeted them in that room over the bed, "we believe in angels." They were so comforted by that, and the coincidences that were occurring all around them. I was still finding feathers all along at home, and whenever we took a trip. My hairdresser joked that Lily joins us and packs her little suitcase of feathers …

July 4 came, and Jacquie and Brian were in Las Vegas with friends. I was sitting outside and got a real sense of Lily out there. I told Dennis since it was the holiday, we should visit her. We made the forty-minute drive to the cemetery with flowers and flags for her. It was about ten in the morning. The phone rang, and it was Jacquie and Brian. It was only seven o'clock in Vegas, so I remember being puzzled why they would be calling us so early.

"We hit the jackpot here; we are pregnant!"

They had done a test there, and it was positive. They figured they were due sometime in the middle of March.

We said, "Guess where we are? We are with Lily!"

Something just told me we had to be there, to apparently share the good news with her. I was thrilled of course, but I have to be honest we were all a little apprehensive about another pregnancy. The thoughts of this happening again did occur, but we all had to put the situation in the hands of God.

After the visit with the doctor later that month, it was determined that Jacquie's due date was March 17, St Patrick's Day. Emerald Isle, the four-leaf clover, and a due date of the luckiest day of the year—God was trying to give all the signs he possibly could to our concerned hearts and superstitious human minds; this pregnancy was going to be okay.

Time marches on, and all through Jacquie's pregnancy, the feathers were still coming. At this point, I decided to count them, and I had close to one hundred! I still always felt excited, humbled, and grateful to be receiving them, and I kept spreading the news of my feather findings. At Lily's grave, Jacquie and Brian spotted one on the edge of the headstone on the grass. That feather remarkably stayed there, literally for months. through our "beautiful" Ohio weather, which means lots of wind and rain. It was a reminder how much she really was watching over us.

The focus was now off losing Lily Jo and sadness, and now onto wonder. God was strengthening my faith and others as well. People were now bringing *me* feathers.

They would say, "Oh, I found a feather and thought of you and Lily. I just had to pick it up and give it to you."

Awareness through something as simple as a feather was amazing! My Facebook friends were now starting to send me articles about feathers being a sign from loved ones above. Beautiful pictures and quotes were so helpful.

I wasn't alone, of course. Others had experienced this gift and had opened eyes and hearts (and mouths) along the way to spread the news. I feel so honored and blessed every day God gave me this gift. We go through life so focused on problems and burdens that we put our blinders on the signs all around us. It took a tragedy to open mine in the way that it had. If I can help even one person cope with their loss, then Lily Jo's death was not in vain. She is our angel and our hope, our "light as a feather."

Jacquie was feeling good, but the doctor was not taking chances and doing ultrasounds very regularly. Everything was looking good. The C-section was scheduled for March 11, 2013. Apparently, they are always performed a week before the actual due date which would have been on my birthday March 10, but it fell on a Sunday, so Monday, March 11 it was! As thrilled as I would have been to share a birthday with this sweet baby, I was only concerned about it being a healthy one.

In the fall, Jacquie and Brian had a "gender reveal" party at a lovely restaurant in Wadsworth. She wanted to celebrate the occasion with friends and family who had been so supportive and loving through their ordeal. It was something to take our focus off the fearful thoughts that were lurking in the back of our minds every now and again, to a happy night of fun.

I went with Jacquie to the bakery, the morning of the party, to pick up the "mystery cake". It was decided that the cake would either have pink or blue icing on the inside and white icing on the outside. The ultrasound technician put the baby's gender in a sealed envelope, and it was delivered to the baker. When the proud parents would cut the cake, the color would be revealed—pink for girl, blue for boy!

We were standing in the line at the bakery behind a gentleman with a little girl. As he talked to her, we both heard him address her as Lily. It was a moment of surprise for us both, but a bittersweet one as well. She was always with us and we both felt she wanted us never to forget her no matter how life was proceeding.

About thirty guests gathered at the party and were given the choice to be on "team pink" or "team blue." Team blue seemed to be the crowd favorite. Jacquie and I both were pretty positive it was a boy from the beginning, just as strongly as we both knew in our hearts Lily Jo was a girl. Maternal instinct, I guess.

The cake was cut promptly at 9:00 p.m., and amid cheers and screams, the icing was *blue*!

Secretly, I think we were all relieved. It was a new beginning. Not that we wouldn't have embraced another baby girl, but there would be no comparisons. This was Lily Jo's brother.

Everyone there was still struck by Brian and Jacquie's strength and grace through all these months. Of course, they were still hurting, and I am sure they had many sad private moments. But all in all, they were doing well and ready for their second child. That became somewhat of an issue in itself. We were unsure of what or what not to say, to people who were not familiar with the situation. All of us were asked, one time or another, if this was a first pregnancy. Depending on the situation, I would explain how we had a "grand angel" in heaven; and other times, it was simply easier not to go into detail. But we always felt guilty taking that route, and did not do that often.

Jacquie was feeling well and had the pregnancy glow. It was December, and she had three months to go. On the ninth, the whole family gathered at the cemetery to celebrate Lily's Jo's birthday. Jacquie and Brian purchased pink balloons for all of us to hold. After saying some prayers and talking to her, we all let them go. The sight of eight balloons rising up was so healing, it was like our sorrow was releasing up to heaven. Of course, two got stuck in the oak tree by her grave, and that was okay; she was looking over us as usual.

I still could not go out and buy blue baby clothes that I knew Dennis wanted to purchase. He lovingly honored my wishes this time. The thirty-sixth-week appointment was nearing and of course, with much apprehension. The doctors and staff had been so accommodating, and Jacquie was, of course, determined to be a high-risk pregnancy from the beginning. They performed many ultrasounds, and in fact, she was very upset if they did not give her one. The number of pictures of her baby boy that hung on the refrigerator were increasing. But unfortunately, there are insurance rulings about how many ultrasounds can be given.

They assured her that all was well, but truth be told, they assured her of that fact during her first pregnancy.

Again, our faith had to be strong, and we had to trust. Luckily, the feathers were still coming.

The thirty-sixth-week appointment went well, thank God. The baby looked good and there was no reason for concern. We all breathed a big sigh of relief, and as human nature goes, the guard goes down just a little when you think all is well.

The next week, the unthinkable happened at her weekly appointment. The ultrasound technician thought she saw the cord around this baby's neck as well. Of course, the office was on high alert, and many doctors in the practice were called in to look closely over and over again at the ultrasound. It was determined that Jacquie should see a renowned specialist from neighboring Akron, Ohio.

How could this be happening again? we all thought.

But you have to go on. You just have to. No matter how scared, angry, and shocked you feel. You have to be supportive as parents, plain and simple. Getting hysterical is not the way to help anyone. Again, our faith put us on "autopilot," and we forged ahead, praying continuously to God and all the angel and saints that this situation would have a positive outcome.

And again, Jacquie and Brian showed incredible strength, by the grace of God.

Since it was the end of February 2013, and the baby was due to be born on March 11, the thought occurred to us, and also from a suggestion from Jacquie's regular ob-gyn doctor, that maybe an early C-section might be the answer.

The appointment with the specialist was scheduled shortly after, and we all made the trip up. After what seemed to be the longest half an hour ever, Brian came out to the waiting room to us to tell the good news that the doctor did not think the cord was wrapped around the baby's neck at this time. Jacquie would be checked again by him regularly. He also did not recommend an early C-Section and was emphatic about that.

As a family we were all torn on the situation at hand. Of course, we did not want to put Jacquie or the baby in harm's way by doing an early C-section, that went without saying, but we also did not want a repeat performance of the cord situation either. As time went on, we felt there was an increased risk that it could happen again. Even as rare as we were assured that would be, it was a very big concern.

The days slowly went by, and my birthday, March 10, was celebrated by all of us. It was the day before the planned C-section, and we all just wanted to be together. It was a lovely evening and helped get the big next day off our minds somewhat. But of course, we both had another sleepless night ...

March 11! The big day finally arrived—nine months of anticipation, fear, prayers by us and others, and countless number of feathers. All the while, we were trying to be calm and live our lives as normally as possible.

Dennis and I arrived at the hospital after the forty-minute drive with anxious feelings. The memory of the trip when Lily Jo died was naturally in our minds. But this time, with anticipation and hope for a normal and healthy baby boy.

We realized when we arrived at the maternity floor that Jacquie was assigned to the same room as when she had Lily Jo. I looked at her with questioning eyes and told her, if it was too hard to be in there, we could request she be moved to another room.

She looked at me and said, "It's okay, Mom, I will be fine."

We had come full circle. We had to trust this time all would work out.

The nurses came to bring Jacquie and Brian to the delivery room. After many kisses, hugs, and words of encouragement, we all nervously watched them go down the hallway. That left Brian's parents, Dan, Dennis, and I to spend what seemed an excruciating long period of time in the waiting room. You try to make small talk, but the time seems endless. Finally, after about an hour, we heard the sound of Brahm's Lullaby playing over the loudspeaker. I was used to this tradition, as the hospital I had worked for in Canton for many years, had implanted this sweet practice of playing the tune when a baby was born. Could it be "ours"? No one came out, so we were all wondering and hoping someone would, soon.

Finally, Jacquie's doctor, who had delivered Lily Jo, appeared. He looked at both grandpas and said, "Jacquie had a healthy baby boy, and he looks like you," and turned to walk away.

Now all the months of anxiousness finally came out in me.

I ran after him and grabbed his arm. "Are you *sure* everything is okay? Are you really, really sure?"

He looked at me with tears in his eyes and quietly said, "Yes, I am sure."

It had been quite a journey for him as well, I realized. He had lost a child too, and we were told that he poured over records to see if he had missed something crucial with Jacquie's first pregnancy. I am sure it was very emotional for him as well.

As I walked back, I saw everyone hugging, shaking hands, and calling on their telephones spreading the good news. I found a glass-enclosed room right beside the waiting room. I couldn't take it any longer. I could not be strong for one more minute. I fell to my knees and sobbed and sobbed. All the emotion that had been balled up inside me, these months of being strong, could no longer stay there. And of course, I had to thank my God.

Dan came in and saw me. "Mom, you okay?'

We hugged for a long time, and I cried some more. And *then*, I was ready to whoop and holler and be a *grandma*!

Brian finally came out, and he, too, told us everything was fine, and we would be meeting Grady James, our eight-pound, nineteen-inch grandson, soon. Words cannot explain the joy and relief when we all met this beautiful and healthy baby who was lovingly being held in his mother's arms. After all the worries and fears, there was no joy that had ever been greater in my life than that moment.

The next days were filled with jubilation, lots of visitors, and a sea of blue gifts, flowers and balloons for Jacquie and Brian. Friends and relatives from all over were so thrilled for all of us. It was a time for love and celebration of a much-anticipated new life. I had mentioned to Jacquie that I missed seeing Joan Marie, our angel nurse, as we were told that she had taken a few days off. I was so disappointed as I would have loved to have shared the joy with the woman who helped us so much with all the sorrow.

But as luck would have it, the day that Jacquie was to be released, in walked Joan Marie! She was dressed beautifully in street clothes, as she had made a special trip to see us. The nurses on the floor had called her, and she was dear enough to come in on her own time. We were all thrilled to see her again, and she too was so happy to see us and meet the baby. She now had come full circle with us. And we found out it was in more ways than one.

She later pulled me aside and then explained to me that after Lily's death, her child had experienced the death of a newborn grandson.

As I looked at her in disbelief, she said, "I admired the grace you and your family had during your difficult time, and I remembered that when we were going through ours."

It was probably one of the nicest things that had ever been said to me, and a moment I will never forget. You never know when you meet someone how your lives will be entwined. There again, the plan God had for all of us, was set in motion. Once again, my "best worst day" had brought something good out of something *bad*. And I am truly touched and humbled by all these experiences.

LIGHT AS A FEATHER

Epilogue

Almost six years have gone by since Lily Jo passed away. I started writing this memoir at least five years ago, but it has taken me so long to make sure the right message and words were conveyed. I have at least three hundred feathers. Since then, Grady is now four and a half and is a talkative, kind, and sensitive boy. He now has a two-year-old sister, Lyla, our beautiful "diva" who loves anything girly and is starting to give Grady a run for his money. He has always been kind to his sister from day one. We can't help but notice, though, when we are taking the kids somewhere special or they are playing together outside, one of us will inevitably find a feather.

I know Lily is saying, "Hey, I want to join in the fun. I am here too!"

Lyla's entrance into the world came in typical Jacquie and Brian fashion—*eventful.*

Jacquie was scheduled for another C-section on Monday, May 4, 2015. I have a tradition of having a Kentucky Derby party the first Saturday in May, whenever possible. It was May 2, and Jacquie, Brian, and then two-year-old Grady arrived all dressed up in their fashionable derby attire. I had a houseful of close to thirty people from in town and out. Everyone was in a festive mood, and the weather was uncommonly warm for May in Ohio. People were inside, and outside on the patio before the race started. Jacquie was feeding Grady in the highchair next to my mother, who never experienced the weird sensation of a pregnant woman's water breaking.

I was busy tending to my guests when a nervous Brian came up to me. "I have got to take Jacquie to the hospital *now,* and please don't tell anyone until we have left."

They had a forty-minute drive back up to the hospital we were so accustomed to and knew that everyone would want to wish them well and hold up the process of them getting out the door! Oh, how I wanted to go with them, but here we were with a houseful of company, and a two-year-old who wondered where his mommy and daddy went.

I took him into the living room where it was quiet, and we settled in to read a book. That was when he looked up at me and said, "Meemaw hat off!"

He probably thought, *You look ridiculous and start acting like my grandma!*

Of course, the nerves for me were on edge—that same old fear comes creeping back in. It was not the way we planned; it was supposed to be a scheduled C-section, not a "here we are" C-section. I was a mess inside again, trying to hold it all together. But don't think I did as good a job this time. I have the best network of family and friends, and again, they were here for us to help us in our time of apprehension.

After about two-and-a-half hours, we got the final call that our sweet Lyla Denise (after her grandpa Dennis) was perfect, and Jacquie was fine too. Again, my prayers were answered. I have to admit, I was mentally exhausted, and the party broke up a little earlier than expected. We had a few good friends stay and help clean up. One of them was someone who used to look at me a little strangely when I would talk about my feathers. But I knew he was trying to be polite and try to understand as well. All of a sudden, I heard him say *whoa* very loudly.

We all looked and saw a large black feather in the middle of the dining area. It was like a crow decided to shed one right there. He looked at me in disbelief as I picked it up and thanked Miss Lily Jo Crescenzo for yet another gift, just at the right time.

I would have liked to have said that I remember each and every time when I found a feather or written each experience down, but I did not. I do remember, though, the feeling of awe, wonder, and love when I did find these treasures. And I would like to share one experience that will stay with me forever.

About three years ago, we were headed to Chicago for the wedding of a dear friend's daughter. We decided to stop on our way at Notre Dame and tour the beautiful campus and visit the grotto. We left the college and decided to have dinner in downtown South Bend. After dinner, we were holding hands crossing a busy intersection when I looked down and spotted a feather in the street. I went to bend down to pick it up.

Dennis said, "You'll have to pass that one up this time. There's too much traffic."

I looked at him and replied, "Lily's not going to like that, and neither do I."

We were back at the hotel when I heard yelling from the bathroom, "Mare, come quick!"

Nervously, I ran in to see what the matter was, and lo and behold, there was a large white feather coming out of Dennis's boxer shorts! Lily was bound and determined we were getting a feather from her that day, traffic or no traffic! It also proves that time does heal our wounds, and somehow, some way, even in tragedy, God does have a sense of humor—and in this case, so does our sweet Lily Jo.

About the Author

Mary Jo Varn is a lifelong resident of Canton, Ohio. She is a retired certified mastectomy fitter. Mary Jo has been married to Dennis for thirty-nine years. She is the proud mother of two children and happy grandmother of two grandchildren, and one grand-angel, Lily Jo.

This is her first book, which she feels has been divinely inspired.

CPSIA information can be obtained
at www.ICGtesting.com
Printed in the USA
BVHW031832270119
538786BV00001B/59/P